AlphaZoo Christmas

This book is dedicated to all the world's animals.
– S.H.

Printed and bound in the United States of America.

Published by Ideals Publishing Corporation
Nashville, Tennessee 37214

Library of Congress Cataloging-in-Publication Data is available.

ISBN 0-8249-8623-7 (trade)
ISBN 0-8249-8632-6 (lib. bdg.)

The illustrations in this book are rendered in watercolors
and colored pencils.
The text type is set in Lower Case Gothic.
The display type is set in Souvenir Light.
Color separations were made by Wisconsin Technicolor Inc.,
New Berlin, Wisconsin.
Printed and bound by Arcata Graphics, Kingsport, Tennessee.

First edition

10 9 8 7 6 5 4 3 2 1

AlphaZoo Christmas

By Susan Harrison

Ideals Children's Books • Nashville, Tennessee

Armadillo
author
addresses
Angora
angels.

B

Boisterous
bluebirds
bake
boysenberry
buns.

Caroling
crocodiles
crunch
candy
canes.

D

Dormouse
duo
dreamily
dozes.

d

Elegant
elk
enjoy
excellent
eggnog.

F

Fireside
foxes
festively
fiddle.

f

Gracious
gecko
gives
guests
gingerbread.

g

Handsome
hares
harvest
holiday
holly.

I

Interested
iguana
impresses
icy
individual.

i

J

Juvenile
jaguars
joyfully
jiggle.

j

Kangaroo
kid
kisses
Kringle.

Leder-
hosened
lemur
lightly
leaps.

1

Musing
mandrill
misses
mate's
mistletoe.

Newts
nibble
nutty
nutmeg
nuggets.

Outspoken
owl
organizes
overland
outing.

Plump
pandas
prepare
persimmon
pies.

Quick-
stepping
quetzals
quiet
quintuplets.

Roving
red
reindeer
raise
ruckus.

S

Sweatered
swine
skate
swirling
spirals.

s

T

Tailored
toads
trade
tiny
teddies.

t

Unsteady
uakari
utilizes
umbrella.

Violet-
vested
vicuna
voices
verse.

Waddling
walruses
wear
warm
woollies.

Xeric
xantusia
x-rays
xenops'
xylophone.

Yammering
yaks
yank
yuletide
yew.

Z

Zestful zebras zippily zigzag.

z